All sorts

Poems by Julia Asling

Cover photos: Stephen Quinn

Body text in Century Schoolbook
Poem titles in **Helvetica Neue bold**

Published by MOJO Media Insights, Brighton, United Kingdom

All poems copyright Julia Asling, 2020

All sorts

Poems by Julia Asling

To Stephen, Magdalena and Mary
with many thanks for their
support and encouragement

Introduction

Many years of teaching English exposed me to the "Great Poets" and filled me with awe. However, being awe-struck does not easily lend itself to the explorations, stumblings and inevitable crashes that are necessary in the process of discovering whether one has "a voice". Or indeed anything new to say.

The passage of time has opened up more space in my life and allowed me the frightening luxury of trying to find out.

About six years ago I came across the line "I write in order to discover what I have to say". This altered perspective freed me and I allowed myself time to try.

The poems in this book embrace many styles from rhyming couplets to prose and haiku. I have loved inhabiting them all and the process has been ongoing and playful.

I hope dear readers you may find in this book of All Sorts some, or a few, that are particularly to your taste and that resonate with your experiences in a way that allows you to see freshly what you already know.

Julia Asling
Brighton, UK
July 2020

In dreams	9
My runaway heart	11
Ode to the Lewes Road	13
What I've learned so far	16
Fallen angel	18
Secret smoking	20
It's Life Jim! But not as we (want to) know it	21
No Self	23
Stories (1)	26
Paris	28
India	31
Monkey	33
Gandhi's glasses	34
Suffolk train	35
Haikus in May	36
Horizons	37
Hindu temple	38
Hindsight	39
What's up?	40
Vampire's kiss	41
The bats	43
A gift	45
Not you	46
Relics	47
Late love	48

A bed of roses	50
Stories (2)	53
Sharpham House (after Yeats)	54
Where we are	55
Boots at Gatwick	56
Surrender	57
Coffee in Casablanca	58
Fighting back	60
Dark matters	62
But I can't leave it there	64

Part 1
To the end of rhyme

In dreams

And sometimes in dreams,
We're all back at the flat.
And I'm fourteen and I'm arsy
And you're biting back.
Then I realise you're dead.
So I cut you some slack.

I don't argue, don't diss you,
I lie down, I retract,
I wanna sooth you, not lose you, again.

And sometimes in dreams,
I'm at Butlin's with you,
There's Nan and aunt Pat, with sweet salty Sue,
I'm playing ping pong,
Or dressed as a witch,
The band is Hawaiian.
The atmosphere's kitsch!
And there are.
Raffles and congas and great knobbly knees,
Rambles and ragtime with clotted cream teas.

But, sometimes in dreams,
You don't answer the phone
And I know that you're missing
And I'm on my own.

When I try to find you,
You're always one step ahead,
Then the truth slips in slowly,
and I know that you're dead.

And in dreams you seem shrunken,
So very pale and so spare
Who back then
Was all knowing, fit, healthy and fair.
The once-open future,
Now lies in the past,
Eternity's endless,
But the tenderness lasts.

My runaway heart

I have so often grappled with my runaway heart,
Over some dark brink or other,
Hauling her back,
Over ice and snow.
Kicking and screaming for cover.
So far we've stayed intact just
But she refuses to play by the rule.
Does she think I'm just downright incompetent?
Does she take me for a fool.

She will not stay.
Be still.
Obey!
And homes in on every abyss or crater
Her willingness to dive right in,
And think about it later,
Astounds me
She is so free
From logic, plan, or reason,
Yet always ready to begin again,
At the start of every season.

She's led me to some far-flung shores.
She will not stay at home
To San Francisco, Delhi and Tehran via Rome.

She took me on the dodgems,
On a roller coaster ride.
She shook me up,
She freaked me out,
She left me gaping wide,
She dragged me into hopelessness so deep,
I thought I'd died.
Then – at the point of giving up.
"Surprise!" she cried, "I lied!"

She sent me to the doctor,
Who prescribed blood-pressure pills,
"Be still and quieten down," he said,
"It'll remedy your ills."
But no can do, she's off again.

Her call I can't ignore.
To stay at home, with my feet up,
Might buy a few years more.
But the real truth is,
That without her,
It'd all be,
such a bore!

Ode to the Lewes Road
(or the street where I live)

Oh, I could've had a pony,
But I chose the Lewes Road
I could've had an Aga.
But I chose the Lewes Road.
I could've had all sorts of things,
A golden crown and angel wings,
But my heart was in the lowlands,
So I chose the Lewes Road.

Oh, Lewes, Lewes, Lewes Road.
Your streets are hardly paved with gold.

In recent days my house caught fire,
The firemen came in five.
I was amazed!
My neighbours all took selfies
As it blazed,
And no one offered health or succour,
The students are all little f&ckers.

But time heals all I hear you cry
And all's forgiven, by and by
We're up and coming, on our way,

There's a new nail bar and a mosque to pray.
An erotic emporium next to the post office lies,
It sells vagina cake and vagina pies.
Pasha de Valentine and Madam C
Invite you in for vagina high tea.
Only hope the postman's letters
Don't get caught up in all the fetters!

Then there's David and Chris
In the corner shop. Bliss!
Why travel afar,
When in search of a jar,
Or an axe or a pin,
(Or even some Omo - cut keys and a bin!)
There's even a tiger tethered out back
For that discerning consumer,
If that, she should lack.
You just can't catch them out,
For they travel about,
Stopping at nowt,
To markets, medinas and cut-price arenas,
To bring us the best at discount.

Oh Lewes Road, you banquet of delights,
Complete with drunks and all-night fights,
Although I may wander life's broad highway,
I will always return and never stray
From the street of my heart,
Till it's time to part
And the Caring Ladies,
Bear me away.

What I've learned so far

Even Lamas wear pyjamas.
Buddhists often get the blues.
Bodhisattvas got their karmas
Sometimes gurus need new shoes.
Oh do it! Do it! Do it now!
Don't ask why and don't ask how.
The animals have got it right,
They sleep all day and they play at night.
They don't borrow money and they don't tell lies.
The fish he swims and the bird she flies.

And so, dear mortals, if you're feeling blue
And those mortgage chains gotta hold on you.
Just look to the cat, she'll show you what to do.

Arch up your back
And howl at the moon,
But just do it with conviction,
Cos it's over oh so soon.

Explode with a bang!
A wallop!
Or a wow!
Do it any way you want to.
But just
Be
Here
Now.

Fallen angel

Hello, hurrah! Let the show begin,
I'm ready!
Hello, hurrah! Let the lights grow dim,
I'm ready.

Angel one enters left,
Rosy crowned and silver winged,
Marks & Sparks Bri-Nylon dress.
Assuming all the piety and purity,
Absorbed from many Sunday Schools,
In damp and dusty vestibules.

A candle burning leads the waves
Of beady eyed and press ganged
Bad tempered, angel slaves.
She loves the music, loves the lights,
In baby Jesus, she delights.

The expectant hush for her, she thinks
And Mummy's smiles and Daddy's winks.
With quavering voice, she reads the verse,
The Shepherds, lambs and Herod's curse.

She wants to stay and stay and stay,
Within the circle of the play.
But, with folded arms and drooping wings,
Half-hearted, Herald Angels sing.

So, she gathers up her gown and glides,
Towards the exit, followed hard behind,
By throngs,
Then trips and screams,
Then slides, then falls.
And hurling curses,
Hits the walls.

And the whole of the path,
to hack an angel shape ...
Worth wearing.

(With thanks to Randy Newman and Sylvia Plath)

Secret smoking

On the yoga course,
Of course!
One does not SMOKE!
And yet,
A habit is hard to resist,
Especially when coupled with G&T,
Drunk from a bottle.
Half pissed.
The devil must have his say.
I have all the gear:
Toothpaste,
Big shell as an ashtray

There must be a way.
Just don't start a bush fire.
They'd never forgive you,
They'd tar you,
They'd feather you,
Put you down, down, down into downward dog
Then they'd hug you,
Then whack you with a bamboo log.

It's Life Jim! But not as we (want to) know it

Whoah! We're all gushing upwards,
Out fresh from the bottle,
Flashing silver and bubbled
Bursting, fizzing, untroubled
By moments past this one,
That contain everything!

Now we're all streaming outwards,
Heading off to strange lands,
Made of coral or treacle,
Look mum, no hands!
Into torments and heartbreaks and erotic blisses
Making marks in the sands
With desires and weird wishes.

Now we're all tumbling over
That rough waterfall,
Falling downwards and screaming
God save us all!
Losing limbs and our senses
Our pearls and our minds.
Then, back in the bottle

With the cork fitted tight.
Farewell to this journey
It's night.
Till next light.

No Self
(Or, Dance me to the end of rhyme)

Well, most of us spend our whole lives
Trying to understand our whole lives.
The sodding, incandescent,
Mystery of it all.
The rise, the fall,
The Well, the Wall,
The Beauty and Feast,
The Buggers,
The Beast
(Oh, don't judge, have a go at rhyming
couplets at least!)
Or, there's trying it out on the others.
The Losers, the Lovers.
Who come onto our paths.
Projections, erections, infections.
The easy (never really easy) laughs.

We're all wounded, we're flying,
We're stealing and buying,
To hide from the thought,
No-one's there to be sought,
Bought, even eventually caught!

No Self, is that elf,
Evading the nets that we shook,
That lets us all,
Off the hook.

In no book, on no shelf,
With great riches or stealth,
Can it be found.
In no mound, nor a sound,
Siren like, spiralling round and around.
Exhausted? Give in?
There's no one
To win.

Part 2
Passing through

Stories (1)

Look. These smooth pebbles,
Lying in my palm,
Are striated,
Rocked by life's forces.
Tightly holding their past.
There are always stories.

They're just concealed behind ordinary exteriors.
At the back of the kitchen drawer.

Is a long-extinct mobile
Charged to cinders
By the longing to hear a voice
Inside that broken camera.

Is still. A snowstorm in Potés,
Filmed from a window
What may occur in time,
To lure them into motion?

Or, on the mantlepiece, captured in a fossil
A two-billion-year-old fish,
Swims toward you, into the room

Graceful, unsuspecting,
Eyes wide open.
Brimming with life.

Paris

Travelling on Eurostar to Paris with you
The sandwich you brought was delicious!
(You cheapskate – yes YOU!)

Walking side by side
Through the Saint Chapelle with you
The lights and the colours
Set the moments and glances
In prisms like jewels
With you.

Then walking arm-in-arm through Paris with you
The bookshops, the clouds and the rain
And haggling for broken umbrellas for pennies
In markets with you.

The Degas dancers in the Louvre,
The stories unfolding in cafes with you.

As we sat in that bar, the shadow came in
Your health problems, bad outlook
But so wanting to win.

So then we spun out there, alone in the blue
Finally, nowhere to go
But with you.

Such ravenous couplings
In lifts and in doorways
So alive! In the darkness
In denial with you.

Going back through the tunnel
Your fear filled the blue
"Let's run away," you said.
But where to. Yes where to.

That summer in London
You shut down, you withdrew
The chemo was brutal
You had to get through
Then you disappeared
Where? Nobody knew.

So I trawled the whole city looking for you.
At last came a phone call
"I'm tired but I'm fine."

Through relief. Disbelief.
I just missed every sign
And then you were gone.

So
Letting go.
Passing on and through
But without you.

India

Three thousand miles in three days,
Traveling through the Punjab.
Milk-white turbans, ruby saris,
Diamonds glinting in the dust.
Places lost in time and mildew.
Empty cafes, filthy rivers.
We're not staying, we're not staying …
Passing through passing through.

Dawn dreaming in Dehradun.
The temple's silver flute wakes up the gods
And breaks my heart.
Long overdue.
Still passing through the dawn's emerging blue.
The Morning Star subsides, subsides from view.

Then, driving through the grey polluted Delhi noon.
The cardboard shacks, the smell of piss.
The begging, indentured helplessness.
I heard Camus said "Poverty is a fortress with the drawbridge up."

So how do you travel through that?
How do you pass through that?
With no return ticket in hand, with no passport back ...

Monkey

Travelling north to Dharamshala
Hoping to see the Dalai Lama.
But he's not there. He's ill in bed,
So we gaze at the monastery wall
instead.
And on the wall a drunk, sad soldier,
Raging, sobbing to a monkey.
Monkey looks, nods, feels his pain.
All we creatures are the same.

Gandhi's glasses

It took three goes
To get to the right Gandhi museum.
"Indira?" *No!* "Nehru?" *No!*
"It is not here," said the tuk-tuk wallah
Beneath a thirty-metre poster of the man.
I went inside.
His glasses were displayed alone.
Polished and slightly bent
In a cavernous case.
And then ...
The story of his life
In miniature wax models.
Starting, oddly, in the middle of it.
Then, weaving back and forth.
Like all of Indian time.
After his violent death at seventy-eight
He returned in the next frame
Alighting from a train
In South Africa, aged about forty.
His tiny wax hand waving.
Still wearing the glasses.

Suffolk train

Passing through the green ribbons of trees.
Saxmundham blue.
Long wide horizons,
Flat fitting earth.
Fierce black band
Bleeding into sky blue
Pearl blue.

Stop. Now. This moment
This is where you live and breathe
This is all you too
Inside, outside – over there
Simply passing through the blue.

Haikus in May

A black crow crowns
The buttercup lake.
Lifting upwards,
Hovering,
Held by the breeze.

She stole the small, dying rabbit
Away from the swarming buzz.
Onto a safe, dry hollow,
Where she stroked him,
Gently away.

Nettle traps between the yellow cups.
Waiting,
For innocent,
Unsuspecting
Flip flops.

Full Dandelion heads
Fall into the grass
Spilling time.

Horizons

There's an unexpected ship on my horizon,
Well, more accurately, a sail.
Without rhyme or reason,
It appeared most suddenly.

The binoculars are still boxed!
This is usually the dry season.
I can't make it out, what could it be?
Much too far away to say,

I wonder, will it break land,
Or crash into the rocks,
Or detour to another cove,
Or just be lost at sea.

Will it raise the Jolly Roger
Or reveal another refugee?

It hovers on the borderline,
Maybe something meant for me
Or merely flotsam,
Scavenged jetsam,
Floating randomly.
We'll see.

Hindu temple

I went to a Hindu temple
Out of curiosity
I observed the rites.
No meat, bare feet and washed.
Then following up the steps
I saw the others pray, into a flickering
light-filled cave.

Then my turn came
To bow, to pray, to crave
But what prayer? I had no prayer.
I looked inside, saw nothing:
A hollowed empty space.
And after, what seemed an infinity of
wait,
A prayer surged upwards from my clean
bare feet
And "Yes," I said. "Oh, yes!"
"YES!"

Hindsight

It's interesting the way things evolved
With that wonky mirror,
Hindsight.

I met you.
Said "No!" too dangerous
Walked away,
But I smouldered and smouldered,
Until my bed caught fire, no, really
So I said, yes.
Then my body caught fire.
"We're alive and it's all good," you said.
Still too dangerous, I thought
But I said Yes.

What's up?

I wanted to send you a note.
I wanted to send you many things.
I wanted to send you my thoughts.
I wanted to send you a hundred things.
I wanted to send you my joy.
I wanted to send you uncounted things.

Then I wanted to give you this poem.
But the ticks on WhatsApp were all grey.
I think that the world's grown too small
For all that I wanted to say.

Vampire's kiss

Beware, oh beware, if your light gets too bright.
There be beasts out there,
Who will feed off your flare.
Once, a vampire bit me
And at first I thought I'd been kissed.
That's the way they do it,
Sweetly, with stealth,
Not with force, or a fist.
They beguile with their charm
Whilst they're planning the harm.
Draw you in with their gaze,
Gently opening the maze.

Enter in at your peril and strife,
For you may not escape with your life!
Oh the mirrors abound and there's scarcely a sound.
Save the beat of your heart,
Rising fear in the chest,
A harmonium's playing
The beast is the best lover
And liar. Don't scream or shout fire.
Or he'll blind you with gas light,
Till you lose all your fight.

Oh, I languished with longing,
While he tightened the leash.
Neither eating nor drinking, devoid of all peace.
Then, in one startling moment, I knew this must cease!
Lashing myself to a nearby mast, off and out to sea I cast.
Throwing away my mobile phone,
So as not to hear the siren's moan.
You have to do it all alone, it seems, in such a plight.
Forget desire, forget the night, forget the fear and fight just fight!
Then keep on swimming,
Towards the light.

The bats

Ebbing peaceful churchyard light
surrounded her,
Sitting smoking on a long flat stone
He joined her
Uninvited
With his laptop
When flying, falling overhead
Tumbling without warning
Came the bats.

Their strong sharp shapes
Pressed hard against the yellow dusk.
Then vanished through the cracks.
She watched and felt the rhythms sweep
the sky
When with a gentle click
A beam of neon sliced her eye
And laptop light spilled everywhere.
As frantic typing cut the silence.
The small bats froze inside the tower
Fragmenting into pixels.

Part 3
Memories and wishes

A gift

What in the world to give
As a gift,
That could be the last?

From the window,
The bushes are bursting with pink roses.
I take a bud,
Slip it into your trouser pocket
Where you may find it later
Searching for a tissue
In the sterile room.

Not you

Sometimes I see your eyes
Glancing sideways,
Passing a stranger along the Esplanade.
Your freckled skin brushes past me
On a random bus journey.
I see your distinctive gait,
Set from years of childhood TB
In the movement of an old man
Next to me in the street.

My heart quickens, my hand
reaches out towards you.
It sharply withdraws as
Reality overtakes my longing
And immeasurable loss
Fills all of me.

Relics

And then we had this.
Unexpectedly, five years after.
In the topmost cupboard, far from reach
inside a Crocodile handbag
What was lost.
Your glasses, ring, gold watch.
Waiting patiently to ambush your wife.
The now small woman.
Her face in bloom,
She slipped out the relics of your life,
She clasped them to her chest
"Oh, there you are," she said.
We both stood in awe.
At your remaining power to reach us.
Still.

Late love

Nearer to the end than the beginning.
What is late love?
The passionate/ blissful/ hurtful
exploration of all the untried feelings?
Do you want them again?
Partly yes!
Mostly no.
What is this new, unsought for
happening?
How to frame it.
An unexpected meeting.
Not online or contrived.
At a party you didn't want to go to,
In a spring you were already weary of,
In a kitchen with bright lights,
Wearing a green dress they all admired!
His form weaved through the crowd
With a glass of wine.
And another and another.
A softly-spoken Sommelier,
Graceful and persistent.
Then, disappearing in the haze.
So, on it whirled.
"I hear you're a poet!"
"Oh really? Am I?"

Snatched conversations
With a dozen others.
Then, at the end,
A napkin, crumpled, with your name and number.
"Call me," it said.
Not knowing what to do,
I waited.
Then, I did.
And now, it unfolds.

A bed of roses

Where am I?
"You're in our bed.
With me my dear,
fifty years we've lain here.
Years racing by,
Where have they gone?
Cup of tea dear?"
Ahh ...
"Here, take your pill dear."

What's that!
"It's just the cat dear.
Remember Puss in Boots?"
Yes. The king ... with a chair.
"Yes, yes. Under the chair.
And Cinderella?"
Shoes, shoes. Ugly, ugly sisters.
"Yes!"
They got blisters. She got a prince.
"She did indeed."

Who's that, in the picture?
"That's our daughter."
*Really? Our daughter?
She found my teeth.*

"She did dear.
And remember Robin Hood?"
Yes! In the forest, in that lake, no clothes on swimming, swimming in the green.
"Yes, we did."
He got the sheriff, helped the poor.

"He did, like you dear."
Me?
"You were shop steward in the union, dear.
Only you walked out when the iron lady's offered hand came near."
Umm.

"And remember the Brownshirts with Mosely in that East-end crowd?
You shouted: 'You're all cowards' with no fear."
Did I?
"Yes!"
Was he a prince?
"Oh, no! No dear."
Who am I?
"Much more than you know, much more … Tea dear?"

Part 4
Light and dark

Stories (2)

Let the stories
Melt.
The stories are just constructs,
In the flux.
When hardened, they take on,
A limited shape
For a time.
They serve the moment
Which is fine.
Till another moment and another
Rhyme intrude,
Which must be honoured,
Or the rhyme, goes round and round
Gathering momentum,
Causing the delusion of
Solidity.
We then mistake for something called
Reality.

Sharpham House (after Yeats)

Turning and turning on the spiralling way,
The receding cupola puzzles the eye.
Domes fall apart.
The centre's a mirage.
Mere illusion is loosed upon the stairs
The lamp lit rooms are dimmed,
The marbled entrance fashioned for effect.
Surely the moonlit lawns aren't lies?
I turn the lock, look back, then go outside
Another room, of space, is bounded by the hills and sky.
The icy pinpricks of the stars,
Glint through its walls.
Orion's belt is on the ridge
It comes, then goes,
(Another trick?)
Recedes, then flickers, strains my eyes.
Stars fall apart.
The nebulas cannot hold,
As white-hot galaxies struggle to be born.

Where we are

After all that turmoil, all those bombs, a new land
Of, if not honey, at least free milk and care for teeth and vaccinations
Against the many plagues.
And spanking, spacious council flats, the trees! The swings!
And street games, really! In the streets.
Then music that seemed loosed from heaven and windows opening everywhere.

When was the point at which it stopped, slowed down, reversed, nose-dived?
All that was given, taken back?
The game was up.
Now came the flack.

A new, New Land, of fear and debt,
Rose up from causes slowly set,
From inattention, apathy,
From lack of care – to all unfair,
From greedy grasping hands.
The plagues are back across the lands.
The milk's gone sour, the flats are let.
The street game's shame.
We're all to blame.

Boots at Gatwick

I went to Boots at Gatwick
To buy a world adapter.
I plugged myself in
The current was so very thin
I could still feel everything.
Unadapted till the end.
I called a friend
To lend a hand, to feed the force.

Answerphone.
Of course!
The assistant said
Just stay in bed and watch the screens,
Lean to the right, the far, far right
Then everything will seem all right
Just slumber through the night
Don't squirm
Ignore the burns
It always turns
Towards the light
Just don't fight
Or you might bite
The hand that feeds you.

Surrender

In this time of standstill.
What.
Where to go.
Why.
Shrunk within this vastness. A small contracted,
Utterly unmoving point.

Which froze first.
The inside
Or outside.

Woven now together.
Into
This cold March evening.
The TV screen flickers
Someone talks
Of Minoan civilisations.
Sitting here, watching,
Unmoved,
By the whole of Western history
I just wait.

Coffee in Casablanca

At the intersection, a shrouded dump
of a city.
Glimpses of past grandeur mingle with
formica.
Moulded Parisian-styled tables.
Are served with steaming coffees.
She appears from nowhere
Beaky nosed, fierce burning eyes
That hold mine for an instant.

Then confidently extending a brown
clawed hand
Takes my sugar cubes and
Slowly put them in her slack mouth –
smiling.
I like her! I grin back at her cheek
You don't get this at Costa.

And then
She's gone! replaced in seconds by a
filthy, one-eyed man
Who shouts accusingly at my coffee.

Snatching the cup
With a theatrical flourish

He swallows hard
Blistering his mouth.

Suspended in that moment
I wonder, will he spit the burning liquid
in my face
With cup to follow?

No! Angry, armed with pots and pans
The cafe staff burst outside screaming
And chase him down the dusty street.

I get another coffee.
Such fury! But not (at all) about the coffee.

Fighting back
(Ode to the times)

But what about the darkness,
That is within me.
I've tried hard, to erase it,
But it will not let me be.
Like Peter Pan's shadow,
That he so needed back.
Let's follow the light,

But what about Black? Yes Black!
At our back.
Fighting and biting, into the flack.
He asked Wendy to mend it,
So he could fly through the night
And beat Hook and his Pirates.
The Lost Boys all tried,
With their strength and their might.

But,
Without shadows, no winning,
Just defeat and a stinging.
So, Wendy sewed it back on and
The boys held on tight.

Then Tiger Lilly stepped forward,
So fiery and bright.
She allied with Wendy and
They gave Hook such a fright,
That the clock stopped its ticking
And slowly, but surely,
They reversed the plight.
And so in the end Hook,
Not Peter,
Walked the plank.
And he ... sank.

Dark matters

Dark matter, light matter, hard matter,
soft matter, feet dancing on matter,
Pitter patter. What's the matter? It all matters.
Because there can be no casting into darkness,
Without firstly God's light.
Because there is no Sound of Music,
Without the third Reich.

No Sweeney Todd,
Without a delicious pie.
Nor truthfulness without its counterpart,
The lie!

No winning, without losing
In the eternal fight
Or famine without feast.
No most without the least.
No lost without the found.
Or silence that contrasts with sound.
And on and on we go, ne'er friend without a foe.

You know it often seems to me,
Oh yes, and no hater without a lover
That "To be or not to be"
Is not the question.

In a dualistic universe
The one implies the other?

But I can't leave it there

Because I have a stance.
Yes, we all go around
In the glittering dance
Of life then death
Maybe life again.

But meanwhile
We all really feel the pain.
Of inequality, poverty, distance.
Rain that falls on all,
The humble and the vain
Whilst trying our best
To remain, relatively sane.

We rise, we fall
Could we finally hear
The call to arms.

The warm and open arms
Not the grasping taking ones
The arms that hold, enfold us
In a common humanity
That feel – at best
We're one.

www.ingramcontent.com/pod-product-compliance
Lightning Source LLC
Chambersburg PA
CBHW062200100526
44589CB00014B/1888